Shattered Youth:

The Overpenalization of Virginia's Young Offenders

By: Luna Blair

<u>**Disclaimer**</u>

This book does not condone criminal acts in any form and does not seek to downplay the crimes committed or the impact these actions have on victims and their families. We recognize that there are no victimless crimes, and the consequences of criminal behavior can be profound and lasting.

The focus of this book is on human rights, advocacy, and the systemic injustices within the legal system, particularly as they pertain to juvenile offenders and those wrongfully accused or harshly sentenced. It is essential to clarify that the discussions within these pages do not speak to the guilt or innocence of any of the cases mentioned. Instead, we aim to shed light on the legal injustices that individuals encounter, the barriers they face within the system, and the need for reform and support.

Our intention is to promote understanding, awareness, and advocacy for those who suffer from the shortcomings of the justice system, emphasizing the importance of compassion, rehabilitation, and the acknowledgment of every individual's inherent human rights.

Table of Contents

Cover Page

Disclaimers

Acknowledgments

Table of Contents

Introduction

Chapter 1: Historical Context

- o   Overview of juvenile justice system history in the U.S.
- o   The shift from rehabilitation to punishment.

Chapter 2: The System in Virginia

- o   Examination of Virginia's Department of Corrections.
- o   Statistics and case studies of youth offenders in Virginia.
- o   Analysis of specific laws that have changed but still affect current inmates.

Chapter 3: Comparative Analysis

- o   How other states handle juvenile offenders.
- o   Success stories from states that have reformed their juvenile justice systems.

Chapter 4: True Stories

- o   Narratives of juvenile offenders who have faced similar injustices.
- o   Highlighting cases where legal reforms did not retroactively affect those still incarcerated.

Chapter 5: Landmark Cases

Chapter 6: Psychological Impact of Long-Term Incarceration

Chapter 7: Keeping Offenders Locked in Prison: The Misconception of Safety

Chapter 8: Advocacy and Reform

Conclusion & Call to Action

Resources for Further Information

References

<u>Acknowledgments</u>

First and foremost, I extend my heartfelt gratitude to the Universe and the Great Spirit for guiding and inspiring this work. Your presence infuses every page with hope and the possibility of change.

I would like to give *special* thanks to the individuals whose stories illuminate the realities of the justice system and the struggle for human rights, both those named and unnamed. Each of you has displayed immense resilience in the face of adversity, and your voices are vital in advocating for understanding and reform:

- **Torie Chishom**, whose experience as a young offender serves as a powerful reminder of the complexities surrounding juvenile sentencing and the dire need for reform.

- **Travis Irvy**, whose commitment to education and personal development, even in the confines of prison, exemplifies the spirit of resilience and the potential for rehabilitation.

- **Skyy Reese**, whose journey sheds light on the challenges faced by those unjustly incarcerated and the importance of advocacy.

- **Chauncy Jackson**, whose story highlights the impact of harsh sentencing on young lives and the necessity for systemic change.

- **Coker Robison**, whose experiences underscore the complexities of navigating the legal system and the profound effects of incarceration.

- **Jose Ortega**, whose resilience in the face of adversity serves as an inspiration for many seeking justice.

- Jermaine Bell, whose journey reflects the need for compassion and understanding in addressing the issues within the justice system.

- Lerico Kearney, whose commitment to personal transformation exemplifies the potential for growth, even under challenging circumstances.

Your stories have been instrumental in raising awareness about the challenges faced by incarcerated individuals and the urgent need for change within our justice system.

Additionally, I keep all those behind bars in my thoughts and prayers, hoping for their freedom and the opportunity to reclaim their lives.

Free my women, men, and children. May we continue to advocate for justice, compassion, and humanity for all individuals affected by incarceration. Thank you for allowing your experiences to be a beacon of hope for others and for inspiring us to strive for a more just and equitable society.

Shattered Youth:

The Overpenalization of Virginia's Young Offenders

The juvenile justice system in the United States was initially established with the understanding that young offenders should be rehabilitated rather than punished. However, over the decades, this ideal has shifted drastically. Today, countless young individuals are facing adult sentences, leading to lives spent behind bars. This book, "Shattered Youth: The Overpenalization of Virginia's Juveniles," explores the complexities and tragedies of juvenile sentencing, focusing on the state of Virginia as a microcosm for nationwide issues.

One poignant story featured in this book is that of Skyy Reese, a young individual from Virginia whose life took a drastic turn when tried as an adult. Skyy's journey through the legal system is a stark reminder of the flaws that persist within our correctional systems. Another key story is that of Coker Robison, who was sentenced at the age of 15. These cases reflect broader societal issues concerning juvenile offenders in the criminal justice system. Both highlight the complexities of sentencing young individuals as adults, particularly the need for reforms that consider the potential for rehabilitation alongside public safety concerns. While their cases differ in specifics, the underlying themes of justice, societal protection, and the responsibilities of young offenders resonate throughout both stories.

Alongside these, we delve into the lives of other juvenile offenders including Jose Ortega, Jermaine Bell, Chauncy Jackson, Lerico Kearney and Torie Chisolm. Each of these narratives highlights the severe consequences of overpenalization and the ongoing struggles faced by those sentenced as adults.

Chapter 1: Historical Context

Overview of the Juvenile Justice System in the U.S.

The juvenile justice system in the United States has undergone significant transformations since its inception in the early 19th century. Initially, the system was rooted in the belief that young people were inherently capable of rehabilitation, a perspective informed by sociological theories and evolving attitudes toward childhood and adolescence.

Early Foundations: The Reform Era

The modern juvenile justice system began to take shape in the late 1800s with the establishment of the first juvenile court in Cook County, Illinois, in 1899. This court was founded on the belief that children should be treated differently than adults due to their age, social context, and potential for change. Pioneers such as Judge Julian Mack argued for separate legal processes for children, emphasizing rehabilitation over punishment. This period marked a shift away from viewing juvenile delinquents merely as criminals and instead recognizing them as individuals in need of guidance and support.

The Rise of the Punitive Approach

As the 20th century progressed, the juvenile justice system began to experience a significant shift, particularly from the 1970s onward. Increased crime rates, particularly in urban areas, along with a societal push for tougher responses to crime, led to a reevaluation of how juvenile offenders were handled.

1. **Public Perception**: During the late 20th century, a rising fear of crime, particularly violent offenses committed by young people, shifted public perception. The idea that youth could be rehabilitated began to be overshadowed by a growing belief that they should be held accountable and face stringent consequences for their actions.

2. **Legislative Changes**: Numerous states began to pass laws that allowed for the transfer of juvenile cases to adult courts, reflecting a more punitive stance on youth crimes. This included the implementation of "get-tough" policies aimed at addressing juvenile delinquency through harsher penalties.

3. **Notable Legislative Acts**: The 1990s saw the passage of several laws, including the Violent Crime Control and Law Enforcement Act of 1994, which encouraged states to enact harsher sentencing for juveniles. Additionally, the implementation of mandatory minimum sentences for certain offenses began to permeate juvenile justice systems across the country.

Current Trends and Implications

The pendulum between rehabilitation and punishment continues to swing in the juvenile justice system. While many advocates push for reforms that return the focus to rehabilitation, the legacy of the punitive movement remains, as evidenced by the number of juveniles being tried and sentenced as adults.

1. **Social Justice Movements**: Recent years have seen a resurgence of advocacy for reforming juvenile justice, emphasizing the need for equitable treatment, the importance of mental health services, and the potential for rehabilitation rather than punishment. Movements aimed at reducing juvenile incarceration rates and preventing youth from entering the justice system have gained momentum.

2. **Judicial Rulings**: Landmark Supreme Court cases in the 21st century, such as *Roper v. Simmons* (2005), which abolished the death penalty for juveniles, and *Miller v. Alabama* (2012), which prohibited mandatory life without parole for juveniles, signify a judicial acknowledgment of the need for modified approaches to juvenile sentencing.

3. **Ongoing Challenges**: Despite the progress made, significant challenges remain. Many jurisdictions still adhere to punitive models, perpetuating cycles of incarceration and

recidivism among youth. Factors such as socioeconomic disparities, race, and access to legal representation continue to influence outcomes within the juvenile justice system.

The historical context of the juvenile justice system in the United States highlights the complex interplay between societal beliefs about youth behavior, the evolving understanding of childhood and adolescence, and the responses of the legal system. As we navigate the contemporary landscape of juvenile justice, it is crucial to learn from past failures and successes to create a system that prioritizes rehabilitation, supports youth in their development, and seeks to rectify the over-penalization that has characterized recent decades. Moving forward, embracing a holistic and compassionate approach that considers the unique circumstances of young offenders remains essential in fostering a more equitable justice system.

Chapter 2: The System in Virginia

Examination of Virginia's Department of Corrections

The Virginia Department of Corrections (VDOC) oversees a range of correctional facilities, including juvenile justice programs aimed at detaining and rehabilitating youth offenders. Although there have been efforts to improve the system, there are significant concerns regarding the treatment of juvenile offenders in Virginia. This examination highlights some of the negative aspects of Virginia's juvenile justice system, including issues of overcrowding, inadequate mental health services, and the overall effectiveness of rehabilitation efforts.

Overcrowding and Facility Conditions

One of the most pressing issues facing Virginia's juvenile justice system is overcrowding in its facilities. Many juvenile detention centers have seen an influx of youth, leading to conditions that compromise safety and effective rehabilitation. Overcrowding can exacerbate tensions among residents, resulting in increased incidents of violence and aggression (Virginia Department of Juvenile Justice, 2022). Reports indicate that some facilities operate at over 100% capacity, making it challenging for staff to manage the needs of each youth properly (National Council on Crime and Delinquency, 2020).The physical environment of these facilities can also be detrimental to the psychological well-being of young offenders. Poor living conditions, limited access to recreation, and lack of privacy hinder the development of a healthy and conducive environment for rehabilitation. As noted by the Virginia Civil Rights Memo, these conditions can create a cycle of trauma that prevents effective behavioral changes among juveniles (Virginia Civil Rights Memo, 2021).

Inadequate Mental Health Services

Another critical issue within Virginia's juvenile justice system is the lack of adequate mental health services for incarcerated youth. Many young offenders come from backgrounds that include trauma, abuse, and mental health disorders. Studies reveal that approximately 70% of youth in the juvenile justice system have at least one diagnosed mental health disorder (Virginia

Department of Juvenile Justice, 2022). However, many facilities are ill-equipped to provide the necessary treatment, leaving a significant gap in care.

The VDOC's mental health services are often criticized for being insufficient, and a lack of trained staff exacerbates the situation. Reports indicate that juveniles frequently do not receive timely evaluations or appropriate treatment plans, which could help address underlying issues relating to their behavior (American Psychological Association, 2021). Without proper mental health support, youth are at an increased risk of recidivism, as untreated issues can lead to continued criminal behavior.

Effectiveness of Rehabilitation Programs

While Virginia has initiated several programs aimed at rehabilitating juvenile offenders—such as educational and vocational training—the effectiveness of these programs has come under scrutiny. Critics argue that many of these initiatives lack sufficient funding and resources, which hampers their success. The overwhelming focus on punishment rather than rehabilitation can lead to a failure to adequately prepare youth for reintegration into society (Virginia Department of Juvenile Justice, 2022).Moreover, the recidivism rates among juveniles in Virginia reflect the challenges of effective rehabilitation. Studies show that approximately 40% of youth released from Virginia's juvenile facilities reoffend within three years (Virginia Department of Juvenile Justice, 2022). High recidivism rates indicate that many young offenders are not receiving the support and training needed to prevent future criminal behavior, highlighting systemic flaws in the approach to juvenile justice.

Transition from Juvenile to Adult Corrections: Challenges and Impacts

The transition from juvenile to adult corrections is a critical juncture in the lives of young offenders. This shift often occurs without adequate support or intervention, leaving many individuals to confront severe psychological challenges exacerbated by their previous experiences in the juvenile justice system. As they enter adult prisons, many youth do not receive the necessary care to address the trauma endured during their formative years, leading to a cycle of ongoing difficulties that have implications not just for the individuals themselves, but for society as a whole.

Lack of Proper Care in Juvenile Facilities

Juvenile facilities are meant to serve a rehabilitative purpose, but many fail to provide the comprehensive mental health care and support that these young individuals desperately need. A significant number of juveniles enter detention facilities with pre-existing mental health issues, often stemming from trauma, abuse, or neglect in their early lives. According to the National Alliance on Mental Illness (NAMI), about 70% of youth involved in the juvenile justice system have a mental health condition, yet many facilities are not equipped to provide the necessary treatment (NAMI, 2021). When these youth age out of the juvenile system without proper care, they often carry unresolved trauma into adult incarceration. They may have experienced isolation, inadequate education, and punitive measures that focus more on punishment than rehabilitation, deepening their psychological distress. This lack of support can complicate their transition to adult corrections, where the environment is even more challenging and less forgiving.

Psychological Impact of Transitioning to Adult Facilities

Entering an adult prison significantly alters the environment surrounding young offenders, subjecting them to conditions that can worsen their mental health. Many youth face the following psychological impacts during this transition:

Increased Trauma: Transitioning to an adult facility can be a traumatic experience itself. Many juveniles report feelings of fear and vulnerability when placed in environments with older, more violent offenders. The potential for violence, intimidation, and exploitation can amplify their traumatic experiences, leading to further anxiety, depression, and post-traumatic stress disorder (PTSD) (National Institute of Justice, 2019).

Loss of Identity and Self-worth: Young offenders may struggle with a sense of identity and self-worth as they transition into adult prisons. The stigma associated with being a convicted felon can lead to a profound sense of shame, exacerbating feelings of hopelessness and isolation. This loss of identity can hinder their ability to engage positively in rehabilitation programs, thus perpetuating a cycle of recidivism.

Difficulty Navigating the Prison Environment: Without the maturity and coping skills required to navigate the complex social hierarchies of adult prisons, young offenders often find themselves instinctively resorting to maladaptive behaviors for survival. This can include joining gangs for protection, engaging in violent confrontations, or resorting to substance abuse—all of which can further harm their psychological well-being.

Why Society Should Care

The ramifications of how society handles the transition from juvenile to adult corrections extend beyond the individual youth and impact the community at large. Here are several reasons why society should be invested in addressing these issues:

Cycle of Recidivism: When young individuals transition to adult facilities without proper care, they are at an increased risk of reoffending. According to the Pew Charitable Trusts, youth who are incarcerated as juveniles are more likely to return to the justice system as adults if their rehabilitation needs are not met (Pew Charitable Trusts, 2015). High recidivism rates contribute to increased criminal activity, which can lead to higher rates of incarceration and strained public resources.

Public Safety Concerns: Individuals who exit the prison system without adequate support and rehabilitation are often left ill-equipped to reintegrate into society, leading to greater public safety concerns. Programs that emphasize rehabilitation can reduce the likelihood of reoffending and enhance community safety by providing young individuals with the tools necessary to lead productive lives.

Moral and Ethical Responsibility: Society has a moral responsibility to support young individuals in their rehabilitation efforts and to recognize that many youth come from backgrounds of systemic disadvantage and trauma. By failing to provide proper care during and after their imprisonment, society perpetuates the cycle of trauma and recidivism, undermining its own social fabric.

The transition from juvenile to adult corrections presents significant challenges for young offenders, particularly those who have not received proper mental health care and support during their formative years. The psychological impact of this transition can be profound, leading to increased trauma, identity crises, and maladaptive coping mechanisms that hinder rehabilitation. Society must recognize the importance of addressing these challenges, as doing so not only impacts the individuals involved but also serves the broader community by promoting safety, ethical responsibility, and social justice.

Youth offenders in Virginia represent a significant concern, especially regarding the transition from juvenile to adult corrections. Recent data shows that approximately 1,200 youths are incarcerated in juvenile facilities across the state, with many facing severe mental health issues and a significant percentage having experienced trauma prior to their incarceration (Virginia Department of Juvenile Justice, 2022).

Case Study: The case of "John Doe" (a pseudonym for confidentiality) highlights the complexities involved with youth incarceration. In 2022, John was sentenced to a juvenile facility for theft and assault. Diagnosed with ADHD and having experienced domestic violence, John's case underscores the need for comprehensive mental health treatment within juvenile facilities. His involvement in counseling programs resulted in improved behavior and reduced recidivism risk, exemplifying the benefits of rehabilitation-focused approaches (Virginia Department of Juvenile Justice, 2022).

Statistical trends indicate a declining rate of juvenile incarceration, with Virginia's overall juvenile commitment rate dropping by 28% from 2015 to 2021 (Virginia Department of Juvenile Justice, 2022). This decline reflects ongoing reform efforts, including the implementation of community-based alternatives to incarceration.

Analysis of Specific Laws Impacting Current Inmates

The Virginia Department of Corrections (VDOC) operates under a legal framework that defines the rights and treatment of inmates, influencing their rehabilitation and reintegration into society. Several specific laws and legislative changes have significant implications for inmates currently serving time in Virginia's correctional system. This analysis will cover key laws affecting parole eligibility, sentencing practices, and the need for reforms to address systemic issues negatively impacting inmates.

1. **Parole Eligibility and Reforms**

Virginia has one of the most stringent parole systems in the United States, particularly following the enactment of the 1995 "Truth in Sentencing" law. This law mandates that inmates serve a specified portion of their sentences before being eligible for parole, effectively removing discretion from parole boards and extending incarceration durations.

Impact: Increased Incarceration Time: Many inmates are forced to serve a minimum of 85% of their sentences, significantly limiting the potential for early release. This law disproportionately affects low-risk offenders, many of whom could benefit from rehabilitation and reentry programs if paroled earlier (Virginia Department of Corrections, 2022).

2. **Psychological and Social Consequences**

Extended periods of incarceration without the possibility of parole can lead to diminished hope among inmates, negatively affecting their mental health and rehabilitation prospects. The lack of incentive to change behavior can foster a sense of despair, which may hinder effective rehabilitation efforts (Virginia Commission on Youth, 2021).

Limitations on Good Behavior Credits

In Virginia, good behavior credits are awarded to inmates who follow prison rules and engage in positive activities. However, changes in policy have tightened the eligibility criteria for these credits, limiting the opportunities for inmates to earn reductions in their sentences.

Impact: Diminished Incentives for Rehabilitation: The restrictions on earning good behavior credits can demotivate inmates, as they feel that their efforts towards rehabilitation are not recognized or rewarded. This can lead to higher rates of behavioral issues and a lack of engagement in rehabilitation programs, as the incentive structures are too limited (Virginia Department of Corrections, 2022).Increased Crowding and Resource Strain: As inmates find it harder to earn parole or good behavior credits, the prison population may increase, leading to even more overcrowded facilities, further straining resources and undermining the quality of services available to inmates (National Council on Crime and Delinquency, 2020).

3. **Mental Health and Addiction Treatment Initiatives**

Recognizing the significant proportion of inmates with mental health and substance abuse issues, Virginia has enacted several laws and initiatives aimed at improving access to mental health and addiction services. However, despite some progress, these initiatives face critical challenges that limit their effectiveness.

Impact: Access to Care: Legislative efforts to increase funding for mental health services within correctional facilities provide essential support for inmates struggling with untreated mental illnesses and addiction issues. However, many facilities still lack sufficient resources, leading to inadequate treatment and support for those in need (Virginia Department of Behavioral Health and Developmental Services, 2022). Ongoing Challenges: The lack of comprehensive mental health care results in many inmates not receiving timely evaluations or appropriate treatment plans. Without proper mental health support, incarcerated individuals are at an increased risk of recidivism, as untreated issues can lead to continued criminal behavior (Virginia Commission on Youth, 2021).

The legal landscape shaping the lives of inmates in Virginia's Department of Corrections reveals significant challenges and gaps. Specific laws regarding parole eligibility, good behavior credits, and mental health support negatively impact the experiences of those incarcerated. While some initiatives have been implemented to improve conditions and promote rehabilitation, substantial reforms are still necessary to create a correctional system that effectively supports rehabilitation and successful reintegration into society. Continued evaluation and reform of these laws are vital for addressing the systemic issues faced by inmates, emphasizing the need for a justice system that prioritizes rehabilitation over punitive measures.

Chapter 3: Comparative Analysis: Virginia vs. Other States in Handling Juvenile Offenders

The treatment of juvenile offenders varies significantly across the United States, reflecting different philosophies and approaches within state justice systems. This chapter explores how Virginia's handling of juvenile offenders compares to that of other states, with a particular focus on states that have implemented successful reform measures.

Virginia: A State of Stringent Policies

Virginia has a history of taking a tough-on-crime stance, even when it comes to juvenile offenders. The state's legal framework often allows for juveniles to be tried as adults for serious offenses, resulting in lengthy sentences that many argue do not consider the unique rehabilitative needs of young people. Specific factors in Virginia's approach include:

- **Higher Rates of Juvenile Transfers to Adult Court:** Virginia frequently transfers juveniles to adult court, where they face the same penalties as adults.

- **Lengthy Sentences:** Many young offenders in Virginia receive long prison sentences, sometimes without the possibility of parole, reflecting a punitive rather than rehabilitative approach.

- **Limited Use of Alternative Programs:** Virginia relies heavily on incarceration, with less emphasis on alternative programs such as community service, restorative justice, or intensive supervision programs.

Comparative State: California

California: Emphasis on Rehabilitation and Restorative Justice

California's juvenile justice system has undergone significant reforms in recent years, shifting from a punitive approach to one focused on rehabilitation and restorative justice. Key components of California's approach include:

- **Proposition 57:** Enacted in 2016, Proposition 57 requires that judges, rather than prosecutors, decide whether juveniles should be tried as adults. This legislation aimed to ensure that more young offenders are kept within the juvenile system, which is more geared toward rehabilitation.

- **Division of Juvenile Justice (DJJ) Transformations:** California's DJJ has shifted its focus to provide more comprehensive education, mental health services, and vocational training to incarcerated youth. These programs are designed to prepare young offenders for successful reintegration into society.

- **Community-Based Alternatives:** California places a higher emphasis on non-incarceration solutions, such as probation, counseling, and community service, which have been effective in reducing recidivism rates.

Success Story:

Nina's Transformation: At 16, Nina was convicted of robbery and sentenced to the DJJ. Through the DJJ's restorative justice programs, she received educational support, vocational training, and therapy. She earned her high school diploma and completed a culinary arts program while incarcerated. Upon release, Nina secured a job in a local restaurant and now mentors other at-risk youth, sharing her story as a testament to the power of rehabilitation over punishment.

California has long been a leader in juvenile justice reform, particularly following the introduction of the "Youth Offender Parole" bill and the "Division of Juvenile Justice Reform." These reforms have aimed to change the trajectory of how juveniles are treated in the justice system.

Diversion Programs: California emphasizes diversion over incarceration. Programs like the "California Blueprint" aim to redirect youth away from detention by investing in community-based interventions that address underlying issues such as substance abuse, mental health, and family dynamics (California Department of Justice, 2023).

Restorative Justice Practices: Many counties in California have implemented restorative justice programs that focus on repairing harm and involving the community in the rehabilitation process rather than punitive measures. This includes victim-offender mediation, which can lead to better outcomes for both the juvenile and the victim (California Board of State and Community Corrections, 2022).

Reduced Secure Confinement: Similar to Virginia, California has reduced its use of secure confinement for juveniles. In 2013, California closed several state youth prisons and moved to a community-based model focused on mental health and educational rehabilitation (California Department of Corrections and Rehabilitation, 2017).

Massachusetts: Progressive Reforms and Youth Development

Massachusetts has also embraced a more progressive approach to juvenile justice, emphasizing youth development and community-based interventions. Key elements of Massachusetts' system include:

- **Raise the Age Legislation:** Massachusetts raised the age of criminal responsibility to 18, ensuring that 17-year-olds are treated as juveniles rather than adults. This legislative change reflects the state's commitment to providing age-appropriate interventions.

- **Positive Youth Development (PYD):** The state's juvenile justice system incorporates PYD principles, focusing on fostering strengths, talents, and potential in young offenders. Programs are designed to develop life skills, educational achievement, and pro-social behavior.

- **Diversion Programs:** Massachusetts utilizes diversion programs to keep youth out of formal legal proceedings, instead offering counseling, mentorship, and educational support. Diversion aims to address the root causes of criminal behavior and promote long-term success.

Success Story:

Jason: Jason, 17, was arrested for a series of minor thefts. Rather than facing incarceration, he was placed in a diversion program that included counseling, mentorship, and community service. Jason worked closely with a mentor, received tutoring, and actively participated in community projects. Within a year, Jason showed significant improvement in his academic performance and behavior, graduating from high school and pursuing higher education. His journey highlights how supportive interventions can reshape the future paths of young offenders.

Success Stories from Reformed Juvenile Justice Systems

Several states in addition to California have successfully reformed their juvenile justice systems by adopting innovative practices:

Texas: Texas has undergone significant reform since the mid-2000s when it shifted from a punitive to a rehabilitative model. The state closed several juvenile correctional facilities and implemented community-based alternatives, resulting in a 40% decrease in the juvenile incarceration rate between 2007 and 2017. Texas now emphasizes treatment and rehabilitation through speciality courts (Texas Juvenile Justice Department, 2019).

Ohio: Ohio has also made strides in reforming its juvenile justice system, focusing on mental health and community services. The state integrated mental health screenings into the juvenile justice process, resulting in better identification of youth needing services. As a result, youth recidivism has decreased by over 20% since the implementation of these reforms (Ohio Department of Youth Services, 2021).

Florida: Florida's "Raise the Age" law, passed in 2019, shifted the age at which youth could be charged as adults. It provided funding for juvenile diversion programs and alternatives to incarceration. This has led to a significant decrease in juveniles being held in adult jails (Florida Department of Juvenile Justice, 2020).

The comparison between Virginia and California reveals substantial differences in handling juvenile offenders, with Virginia gradually moving toward rehabilitation and California leading in innovative diversion and restorative justice practices. States like Texas, Ohio, and Florida further exemplify successful reform efforts that prioritize rehabilitation, community-based services, and reductions in incarceration rates. These reforms not only improve outcomes for juvenile offenders but also create healthier communities by addressing underlying issues rather than merely punishing behavior.

Lessons for Virginia

Virginia can draw valuable lessons from the successes of states like California and Massachusetts. Here are several recommendations based on the comparative analysis:

1. **Reevaluation of Juvenile Transfers to Adult Court:** Virginia should consider legislative changes similar to California's Proposition 57, requiring judicial oversight for decisions to try juveniles as adults. This shift can ensure more appropriate handling of juvenile cases within the juvenile justice system, focused on rehabilitation.

2. **Expansion of Rehabilitation Programs:** Implementing more comprehensive rehabilitation programs akin to California's DJJ transformations can provide young offenders with the tools they need for successful reintegration. Emphasizing education, vocational training, and mental health services can prepare juveniles for a positive future.

3. **Investment in Community-Based Alternatives:** Virginia could benefit from adopting Massachusetts' approach to diversion programs and Positive Youth Development (PYD) principles. Offering alternatives such as mentorship, counseling, and community service can address the underlying causes of criminal behavior and promote long-term success.

4. **Raise the Age Legislation:** Raising the age of criminal responsibility to 18, as Massachusetts has done, can ensure that older teenagers are treated within the juvenile system. This approach acknowledges the developmental differences between juveniles and adults, focusing on age-appropriate interventions.

5. **Restorative Justice Practices:** Embracing restorative justice practices can foster accountability, healing, and reconciliation for both victims and offenders. Programs focused on mediation, victim-offender dialogue, and community reparations can reduce recidivism and encourage positive behavioral change.

Chapter 4: True Stories

Chauncy Jackson

On September 1, 1994, 16-year-old Chauncy Jacob Jackson was arrested and incarcerated on charges of capital murder and five other felonies. Having reached his 16th birthday only six weeks prior to the offenses, Jackson became one of the youngest individuals to face such severe charges. Since 1987, ten 16-year-old offenders have been convicted of capital murder, yet Chauncy remains the only defendant among them to receive a death sentence.

Legal Proceedings

The legal journey that followed his arrest was fraught with challenges. On September 21, 1994, the Norfolk Juvenile and Domestic Relations District Court issued transfer orders, determining that Jackson would face criminal proceedings as an adult. This pivotal decision set a trajectory for his life that would forever alter his future.

On October 5, 1994, Jackson was indicted in circuit court on six serious charges:

The capital murder of Ronald Gene Bonney, Jr., while attempting to rob him (Code §§ 18.2-31(4), 18.2-10).

Attempted robbery (Code §§ 18.2-58, 18.2-26).

Use of a firearm during the capital murder (Code §§ 18.2-53.1, 18.2-10).

Use of a firearm during the attempted robbery (Code §§ 18.2-53.1, 18.2-10).

Conspiracy to commit robbery (Code § 18.2-22).

Possession of a firearm by a person under age 18 (Code § 18.2-308.7).

Chauncy Jackson's case highlights the extreme measures taken against juvenile offenders, especially in capital murder cases. The severity of his sentencing raises critical questions about the broader implications of imposing such harsh penalties on young people, especially when considering their developmental stage and the potential for rehabilitation. Despite the formidable challenges he faced, Chauncy has transformed his life while incarcerated. He has become a mentor among the gang community in prison, using his experiences and insights to guide younger inmates who may find themselves caught in similar cycles of violence and crime. Recognizing the need for constructive change, he leverages his position to foster reconciliation and encourage personal growth within the often hostile prison environment.

In addition to his role as a mentor, Chauncy has also embraced a creative outlet: he has become a published author. Through writing, he channels his experiences and emotions into stories that resonate with others. His work reflects his journey of transformation, his struggles, and the lessons he has learned along the way. By sharing his narrative, he hopes to inspire other young people, both inside and outside of prison, and to shed light on the realities of life as a juvenile offender navigating the adult criminal justice system.

Chauncy Jackson's journey raises important ethical and rehabilitative questions regarding the treatment of juvenile offenders within the justice system. The decision to try juveniles as adults, particularly in cases involving capital murder, highlights systemic issues that call for reevaluation. The harsh penalties imposed on young offenders not only affect their futures but also have lasting impacts on their families and communities.

Juveniles are still in critical stages of development, grappling with impulses and decision-making abilities that differ significantly from adults. The justice system's focus on punitive measures often overlooks the potential for rehabilitation and growth, leading to cycles of recidivism and prolonged suffering for both offenders and their loved ones. Chauncy's case emphasizes the need for a justice system that prioritizes rehabilitation over retribution and considers the complexities surrounding young offenders.

Skyy Reese

Skyy Reese's journey through the juvenile justice system serves as a profound example of the sometimes-harrowing path young offenders must navigate. At just 16 years old, Skyy found himself embroiled in a serious legal situation alongside two friends, ultimately leading to their conviction for robbery and abduction. Despite his youth and the context of his actions, Skyy was handed a staggering sentence: 144 years in prison, with 94 years suspended. This left him staring into the abyss of a 50-year prison term in an adult facility—an almost unimaginable reality for someone so young. The severity of this sentence raises critical questions about the appropriateness of treating juvenile offenders as adults and the long-term implications such decisions can have on their lives. Many studies indicate that juveniles are not fully developed decision-makers and are particularly prone to impulsive behavior influenced by their environment (National Institute of Justice, 2019). Skyy's case exemplifies the extreme penalties imposed on youth and the need for a re-evaluation of how the justice system addresses young offenders.

The Discovery of a Plea Deal

Over a decade into his long sentence, Skyy made a shocking discovery: he had been offered a plea deal prior to his trial, one that he was completely unaware of at the time. This plea deal could have significantly altered the trajectory of his life, potentially allowing for a much lighter sentence or the opportunity for rehabilitation rather than a life behind bars. This revelation not only highlights the often-overlooked legal complexities faced by juvenile defendants but also casts doubt on the fairness of the justice proceedings in his case. It raises alarms about the lack of sufficient legal counsel and the awareness provided to young individuals during such critical moments of their lives. The ramifications of this discovery extend beyond Skyy himself; they signify a systemic issue within the juvenile justice system, wherein young defendants, sometimes lacking adequate representation, may not understand their rights or the full scope of available options that could prevent severe outcomes like those Skyy faced.

Resilience and Personal Development

Despite the harsh realities of incarceration, Skyy displayed extraordinary resilience and a commitment to self-improvement. Since his conviction, he has embraced educational opportunities within the prison system. Skyy earned his GED and actively pursued college coursework, showing an unyielding dedication to personal growth. With each class taken and certification earned, he not only developed critical skills but also brought an element of hope and purpose into his life behind bars. He also participated in work assignments when available, which allowed him to gain practical experience and maintain a semblance of normalcy amidst the upheaval of prison life.In addition to his educational accomplishments, Skyy has emerged as a mentor within the gang community in prison. Understanding the rampant cycles of violence and incarceration that plague many young offenders, he has leveraged his experiences to guide and support fellow inmates. By sharing the lessons he has learned, Skyy has helped others navigate the challenges of prison life, promoting conflict resolution and encouraging personal accountability. His mentorship reflects a deep commitment to fostering positive relationships and guiding others toward constructive paths, transforming his once destructive presence into one of hope and guidance.

Skyy's efforts culminated in a significant achievement: becoming a published author. This accomplishment is a powerful testament to his potential for transformation and illustrates that even within the confines of prison, individuals can strive for greatness and contribute positively to society.

Broader Implications for the Juvenile Justice System

Skyy Reese's narrative goes far beyond his personal triumphs; it serves as a reflection of broader issues within the juvenile justice system. His experiences underscore the complexities and severe consequences of sentencing young individuals as adults. The case casts light on how the legal system often overlooks the inherent potential for rehabilitation in juvenile offenders. Instead, it frequently opts for harsh punishment, disregarding the possibility of reform and the long-term benefits that come from investing in young people's futures.

Skyy's story is emblematic of the urgent need for systemic reforms that balance the imperative for public safety with the understanding that young people are capable of significant change. Many advocates argue for policies that focus on restorative justice and rehabilitation rather than retribution, particularly when it comes to juvenile offenders. Redirecting focus can not only improve the lives of individuals like Skyy but also foster healthier communities by reducing recidivism rates and promoting successful reintegration.

Coker Robison

Coker Robison was just 15 years old and living on the south side of Richmond when, in 2008, he made the ill-fated decision to join three friends in a robbery at a nearby apartment complex. Robison provided one of the accomplices with an unloaded BB gun pistol, which was also missing its CO_2 cartridge. The group, all wearing face coverings, executed their plan, entering the home through the front door after a knock was answered while Robison stationed himself at the back door.

In less than a minute, when the back door swung open, Robison briefly stepped into the residence and was handed some wallets, cash, and a cell phone before all four fled the scene. However, within 20 minutes, police tracked down Robison at his apartment, where he confessed to his involvement in the crime. While two of the accomplices managed to escape, the 19-year-old Leon Brown, one of the group, was arrested alongside Robison.

Initially, Robison was charged in Juvenile and Domestic Relations Court with a single count of robbery and a gun-related charge due to his age. However, he turned down a plea deal offered by prosecutor Kelli Burnett, who later opted to try him as an adult. Instead of the two original charges, Robison faced an overwhelming total of 16 felony counts. Ultimately, at just 16 years old, Robison received a harsh sentence of 33 years in prison for a crime in which no one was injured.

Incarceration and Denial of Pardon

Despite his youth and the non-violent nature of the crime, Robison's journey through the justice system has been fraught with challenges. After four years of fighting for a conditional pardon, he received an unsigned letter from the former Office of the Secretary of the Commonwealth and the Pardons Department stating that his request had been denied. This rejection underscores the stringent and often unforgiving nature of the current system, particularly for young offenders. As a result, Robison remains incarcerated in the Virginia Department of Corrections and is ineligible to apply for another pardon until the end of 2024.

Role as a Tutor and Mentor

While Coker Robison continues to serve his lengthy sentence, he has taken significant steps toward personal growth and rehabilitation. He has become an active tutor, helping many fellow inmates prepare for their General Educational Development (GED) tests. Recognizing the importance of education as a pathway to redemption, Robison dedicates his time to guiding others through their studies, offering them the support and resources they need to succeed.Robison's commitment to tutoring demonstrates his understanding of the transformative power of education. By helping fellow inmates obtain their GEDs, he not only provides them with valuable academic skills but also instills a sense of hope and purpose within a challenging environment. His efforts serve as a reminder that, despite the circumstances that led to incarceration, redemption is possible through the pursuit of knowledge and the willingness to support others.

Coker Robison's story reflects the complexities of youth justice and the often harsh realities faced by young offenders in the legal system. Convicted for his role in a non-violent crime, Robison's lengthy sentence highlights the challenges of navigating a system that does not always account for age or potential for change. Nevertheless, his journey does not end with his incarceration. By becoming a mentor and tutor to other inmates, Robison demonstrates that even within the confines of prison, individuals can reclaim their dignity and purpose. His story is a testament to the resilience of the human spirit and the critical role that education plays in fostering hope and redemption, even in the most challenging circumstances.

Jose Ortega

Jose Ortega's story is emblematic of the struggles faced by many young offenders in America. Born and raised in a challenging environment, Jose was the oldest child in a family marked by hardship. His mother, an immigrant from the Dominican Republic, worked tirelessly to provide for her family amidst the financial constraints of their impoverished neighborhood. The absence of his father, a black man who was not part of Jose's life, compounded the challenges he faced growing up. This lack of a paternal figure often left Jose to navigate the complexities of adolescence without guidance, support, or role models who could help him make positive choices.

Growing up in an economically disadvantaged area meant that Jose was frequently exposed to crime and its temptations. The pressures of his environment, coupled with a deep-seated desire to assert his identity and support his younger siblings, led Jose down a path that ultimately resulted in his involvement in criminal activities. At the age of 16, he was convicted of robbery and abduction, a serious offense that would alter the course of his life forever.

Sentencing and Its Implications

Jose Ortega was sentenced to life in prison plus additional time as a minor for the crimes he committed and remains incarcerated while his co-defendants have been released. This severe punishment, which reflects the growing trend across many states to impose harsh penalties for juvenile offenses, raises critical questions about the justice system's approach to young offenders.

Disproportionality in Sentencing: At just 16, Jose faced a punishment that not only stripped away his youth but also condemned him to a life behind bars for actions that may have been significantly influenced by his environment and circumstances. This calls into question whether the criminal justice system is equipped to consider the complexities surrounding juvenile offenders, especially those from disadvantaged backgrounds.

Effectiveness of Harsh Penalties: Studies show that imposing severe penalties on young offenders does not necessarily lead to lower recidivism rates. The rationale behind such harsh sentences is often predicated on deterrence; however, many experts argue that it is ineffective given that young people are still developing their decision-making abilities and are often more impulsive. The harsh punishment deprived Jose of the opportunity for rehabilitation, guidance, and the chance to create a positive future, which could have benefited both him and society in the long run (National Institute of Justice, 2021).

Long-term Consequences: Jose's life sentence not only affects him but also his family and community. With his mother struggling to make ends meet and the absence of a father figure, the burden of his incarceration falls heavily on his younger siblings, who will have to navigate their lives without an older brother. This further perpetuates the cycle of poverty and crime that many families face, creating a ripple effect that can harm entire communities.

Current Role and Support System

Despite being incarcerated, Jose Ortega continues to play a vital role in supporting his family and particularly his younger siblings. He has become a source of emotional strength and guidance for them, utilizing the lessons he has learned through his experiences to offer wisdom and encouragement. His commitment to his family exemplifies his desire to protect and uplift them, even from behind bars.In addition to his familial support, Jose has taken on a proactive stance in the prison environment by engaging in educational initiatives. He has worked to help fellow inmates pursue their education, focusing on literacy and skill development. This involvement has allowed him to foster a sense of community and hope among those he interacts with, showcasing that his spirit remains unbroken despite the challenges of incarceration.

Broader Implications

Jose Ortega's case exemplifies broader systemic issues within the juvenile justice system in the United States. The intersection of race, economic disadvantage, and familial instability plays a significant role in shaping the lives of young people. For example, youth from minority backgrounds, particularly those who are Black or from immigrant families, often face harsher penalties than their white counterparts for similar offenses, revealing potential biases within the justice system (American Civil Liberties Union, 2019).

Furthermore, Jose's story invites a critical examination of alternative approaches to juvenile justice. Programs that focus on restorative justice or rehabilitation rather than strict punishment have shown promise in substantially reducing recidivism rates among young offenders. These programs emphasize personal accountability, healing, and skill-building, providing a more constructive path forward for youth like Jose, who may have made grave mistakes but still possess the potential for change.

Jermaine Bell

Jermaine Bell was convicted for his involvement in the tragic death of 3-year-old Taylor Ricks, a case that shocked the community and raised difficult questions about accountability in the justice system. The incident occurred when Taylor was innocently playing in her home located in the 100 block of Hough Avenue. On that fateful day, she heard what she believed were fireworks, prompting her to peek out the window. Tragically, she was struck by a single bullet fired from a semi-automatic rifle during a shootout outside her home, resulting in her untimely death at the hospital.

In the eyes of the law, the prosecution contended that even though Jermaine Bell did not fire the fatal shot, his actions made him as culpable as the individuals who did. Testimony during the trial revealed that Bell was the driver during a significant portion of the crime, actively participating in the events that led to the chaos and violence. This case exemplifies the complexities of determining accountability when multiple parties are involved in a criminal act and highlights ongoing societal dilemmas about justice and culpability in cases of gun violence.

Incarceration and Transformation

Despite the gravity of the crime with which he is associated, Jermaine Bell continues to serve his sentence and is currently incarcerated. However, his time in prison has not been without purpose or personal growth. Over the years, he has transformed his experiences into a platform for redemption and mentorship. Bell has become a role model and an inspiration to other prisoners, exemplifying how individuals can strive for positive change despite the circumstances of their convictions.

Jermaine has taken it upon himself to create a support system for fellow inmates, offering guidance and encouragement to those who may be struggling with similar feelings of regret, hopelessness, or lack of direction. His ability to connect with others through shared experiences and understanding has made a significant impact on those around him. He has emerged as a beacon of hope, emphasizing the importance of personal accountability and the possibility of redemption.

The Role of Mentorship in Rehabilitation

Bell's role as a mentor within the prison system underscores the value of peer support among incarcerated individuals. Research has shown that mentorship can significantly affect the rehabilitation process, providing inmates with the motivation to engage in positive behavior and pursue educational or vocational programs. Jermaine's efforts highlight that even in the darkest of circumstances, individuals can find purpose and contribute positively to their environment. Through various programs, Jermaine has facilitated discussions around critical issues such as making choices, understanding consequences, and working toward rehabilitation. He has also participated in education initiatives that help prepare inmates for successful reintegration into society, emphasizing skill-building, emotional intelligence, and conflict resolution.

Lerico Kearney

Lerico Kearney has spent more than two decades incarcerated, having been sentenced in 1997 for murder at the young age of 18. His case serves as a poignant example of how the justice system can sometimes fail individuals, particularly young men from disadvantaged backgrounds, leading to prolonged sentences that raise questions about fairness, rehabilitation, and the potential for redemption. Lerico's troubles began in an environment that many would deem challenging. Growing up in Virginia, he faced numerous obstacles, including the absence of solid support systems. The circumstances surrounding his arrest and subsequent conviction are complex, involving a range of factors that contributed to his legal troubles. Notably, Lerico's conviction for murder was achieved without any physical evidence tying him to the crime, a detail that underscores significant concerns about the integrity of the legal proceedings.

The Conviction

In 1997, Lerico was convicted and sentenced to life in prison. The absence of physical evidence in his case raises critical questions about the appropriateness of the conviction and the efficacy of the prosecution's arguments. His case has gained attention over the years as it highlights broader issues within the criminal justice system, including the challenges of adequate legal representation and the application of justice in cases that may involve racial bias or systemic inequities.

In a powerful interview with Jason Flom on iHeart Radio, Lerico discussed his experiences within the legal system and the ramifications of his sentencing. He expressed feelings of abandonment and frustration, speaking candidly about how his youth and the pressures of his environment played a role in his actions. Lerico also highlighted the systemic challenges that individuals like him face, including the lack of access to quality legal counsel and the pervasive issues of racial inequality in the justice system.

Torie Chishom's story is emblematic of the complexities and challenges facing juvenile offenders within the criminal justice system. At just 15 years old, Torie was involved in a robbery that led to charges of four counts of armed robbery, use of a firearm, and malicious wounding. Torie's case highlights the often harsh realities for young individuals in the legal system, particularly as he was tried as an adult—a decision that would drastically alter his life trajectory.

In Virginia, the decision to charge a juvenile as an adult can have devastating consequences. In Torie's case, this punitive approach culminated in a lengthy prison sentence of 47 years, which not only confined him to prison but also separated him from his family and two children. The ramifications of this decision resonate deeply in his life, as he grapples with the continuous reality of missing pivotal moments in his children's lives due to his incarceration.

The approach taken with juvenile offenders often overlooks their potential for change and growth. Studies have shown that young individuals are still developing both emotionally and cognitively, and punitive measures frequently fail to recognize this critical aspect of adolescent development. Unfortunately, Torie's experience illustrates how the legal system can impose harsh penalties that hinder a young person's ability to rehabilitate and reintegrate into society.

Pardon and Continuing Incarceration

Over the years, Torie has sought to advocate for himself and others in similar situations. His efforts culminated in a pardon—an acknowledgment of his potential for reform and a chance for reintegration into society. However, despite receiving a pardon, Torie remains incarcerated, highlighting the complexities and limitations of the justice system. His case serves as a sobering reminder that a pardon does not automatically lead to release.

Even with the formal recognition of his potential to change, Torie's continued incarceration signifies a system that still lacks the elasticity and responsiveness required to address the nuances of individual cases. His situation underscores a critical gap in policy and practice; many individuals like Torie experience significant challenges even after achieving a pardon.

Impact on Family

The impact of Torie's incarceration extends beyond himself to his two children, whose lives he is missing. The absence of a father figure during their formative years creates emotional and psychological challenges for both Torie and his children. As he reflects on the experiences and milestones he has missed, the strain of his absence weighs heavily on him, reinforcing the cyclical nature of incarceration, where the consequences permeate familial and community relationships. His story underscores the importance of understanding the broader implications of juvenile sentencing. The separation of children from their parents due to punitive measures imposes lasting effects on families and communities, perpetuating cycles of trauma and disconnection.

Travis Irvy

Travis Irvy's story is a poignant illustration of the consequences of juvenile sentencing in the adult criminal justice system. In November 2006, at just 16 years old, Travis was involved in a non-murderous crime that led to his conviction and sentencing to an extraordinary 64 years in adult prison. This case highlights the profound implications of lengthy sentences for young offenders and raises critical questions about justice, rehabilitation, and the potential for reintegration.

The Conviction

Travis was charged with several offenses related to a robbery, a crime that, while serious, did not involve murder. Despite this, the decision to try him as an adult resulted in a harsh sentence that deprived him of his youth and opportunities for growth. Under Virginia law, the automatic transfer of juveniles to adult court can lead to disproportionately severe penalties, particularly for individuals like Travis, who were still in their formative years. The lengthy sentence imposed on Travis reflects a punitive approach to justice that overlooks the developmental differences between adolescents and adults. Research shows that young people are still undergoing significant emotional and cognitive development, which can influence their decision-making and behavior. By sentencing Travis to 64 years, the system effectively disregarded his potential for rehabilitation and change.

Life in Prison

Since his incarceration, Travis has faced the many challenges inherent in the adult prison system. However, he has also taken proactive steps to make the most of his situation. Over the years, Travis has completed numerous programs aimed at personal development, education, and skill-building. His dedication to self-improvement and growth exemplifies the resilience often found in young individuals navigating the complexities of incarceration. As a GED tutor, Travis plays a pivotal role in supporting fellow inmates in their educational journeys. His commitment to education not only fosters a sense of purpose but also empowers others to seek opportunities for personal advancement and growth. By helping others achieve their academic goals, Travis contributes to a more constructive prison environment and proves that rehabilitation is possible, even within the confines of a correctional facility.

The Ongoing Impact

Despite his significant achievements and personal growth, Travis remains incarcerated, serving the lengthy sentence imposed upon him at such a young age. His case illustrates the broader issue of how the justice system often fails to recognize the potential for redemption among juvenile offenders. Travis's continued imprisonment raises questions about the effectiveness of punitive sentencing, particularly for non-murderous crimes.

Chapter 5: Landmark Cases

Miller v. Alabama (2012)

Miller v. Alabama centers around the constitutional debate regarding the sentencing of juvenile offenders. The case arose from the conviction of Evan Miller, a 14-year-old who, along with another minor, was implicated in the fatal beating and burning of a man in Alabama in 2003. Charged with capital murder, Miller was found guilty and sentenced to mandatory life imprisonment without the possibility of parole (LWOP). This sentencing was imposed without consideration of his age, maturation level, or the circumstances surrounding his actions, which included significant factors like his troubled upbringing and history of abuse.

Supreme Court Decision

The case was brought before the U.S. Supreme Court, where it was argued that sentencing juveniles to life without parole constitutes cruel and unusual punishment, in violation of the Eighth Amendment. The Court decided on June 25, 2012, and held the following:

1. Cruel and Unusual Punishment: The Supreme Court ruled that mandatory life sentences without parole for juveniles are unconstitutional. The decision was primarily grounded in the recognition that children are fundamentally different from adult offenders in several respects, including their immaturity, susceptibility to peer pressure, and greater capacity for change. The Court emphasized that this distinction should influence sentencing decisions.

2. Individualized Sentencing: The ruling stressed the importance of considering the offender's individual circumstances. Justice Elena Kagan, writing for the majority, articulated that sentencing for juveniles must reflect their unique traits and the lessened culpability attributed to their age. Therefore, courts must evaluate a juvenile's background, the nature of the crime, and their potential for rehabilitation during sentencing.

3. Precedent and Context: This decision built on the precedent set by Roper v. Simmons (2005) and Graham v. Florida (2010), which both recognized the inherent differences between juvenile and adult offenders. These cases contributed to a growing understanding that devices in the juvenile justice system need to account for developmental science and the capacity for reform.

Impact of the Ruling

The Miller v. Alabama ruling had a profound impact on juvenile sentencing across the United States:

1. Reassessment of Sentences: Following the decision, numerous individuals sentenced under similar mandatory laws became eligible for resentencing. Courts across the country began to revisit cases where juveniles had been sentenced to LWOP, providing opportunities for reconsideration based on the new legal standards set forth by the Court.

2. State Legislation Changes: The ruling prompted many states to reconsider their laws around juvenile sentencing. Some states passed legislation to prohibit mandatory life sentences for juveniles, while others instituted guidelines to ensure that sentencing reflects a balanced assessment of the offender's youth and potential for rehabilitation.

3. Reform Advocacy: The case spurred advocacy groups and legal experts to push for broader reforms in the juvenile justice system, emphasizing rehabilitation over punishment. It highlighted a growing recognition that juveniles possess the capacity for change and redemption, thus arguing for a more rehabilitative approach that promotes restorative justice.

Miller v. Alabama significantly advanced the cause of juvenile justice reform in the United States. By establishing that mandatory life sentences without parole are constitutionally impermissible for juveniles, the Supreme Court underscored the importance of considering a young offender's potential for rehabilitation and the unique circumstances that influence their behavior. This landmark case further reinforced the principle that the juvenile justice system should focus on redemption and reform, embracing an understanding of the developmental differences that separate children from adults. The decision has since played a crucial role in shaping ongoing discussions about appropriate sentencing and treatment for young offenders across the nation.

2. Louisiana v. Montgomery (2016): A Significant Ruling in Juvenile Justice

Background

Louisiana v. Montgomery revolves around the implications of the Supreme Court's previous decision in Miller v. Alabama (2012), which ruled that mandatory life sentences without the possibility of parole for juvenile offenders are unconstitutional due to the Eighth Amendment's prohibition against cruel and unusual punishment. The case specifically addressed the question of whether this ruling should be applied retroactively, allowing previously sentenced individuals the chance to challenge their sentences.

The petitioner, Marlon Montgomery, was 17 years old at the time of his conviction for murder in Louisiana. He received a mandatory life sentence without parole. Following the Miller decision, Montgomery sought to have his sentence reconsidered under the claim that it violated the principles established in that case.

The Supreme Court Decision

On January 25, 2016, the U.S. Supreme Court issued a unanimous decision stating that the rule established in Miller v. Alabama should indeed be applied retroactively. The Court ruled that:

1. **Retroactivity of Miller**: The decision clarified that juveniles who were given mandatory life sentences without parole prior to the Miller ruling are entitled to a hearing to determine whether they should be resentenced. This retroactive application is relevant not only to Montgomery but also to all individuals in similar situations across the country.

2. **Emphasis on Rehabilitation**: The ruling reinforced the idea that a sentence for a juvenile must account for their age and the potential for rehabilitation. The justices indicated that the justice system must allow for individual assessments of the offender's maturity, character, and prospects for reform.

3. **Legal Precedent and Impact**: The Court's decision in Montgomery built on the evolving legal landscape regarding juvenile sentencing. It emphasized the necessity of treating juveniles differently from adults in the justice system, recognizing their developmental differences and the inherent potential for change.

Implications of the Ruling

The Louisiana v. Montgomery decision had far-reaching consequences for the juvenile justice system:

1. **Resentencing and Reviews**: After this ruling, many states were compelled to review cases involving juveniles sentenced to life without parole. This led to a wave of resentencing hearings

for individuals whose sentences were affected by the Miller decision, allowing them to present evidence regarding their personal circumstances and potential for rehabilitation.

2. **Judicial Guidelines**: The ruling has had implications for how judges approach sentencing for juveniles. Courts needed to establish procedures that consider a juvenile offender's character, family history, and the role of peer pressure, among other factors, in determining appropriate sentences moving forward.

3. **Reform Movements**: Montgomery's case further fueled advocacy efforts aimed at reforming sentencing laws for juvenile offenders across the United States. Activists and legal experts engaged in discussions about the importance of rehabilitation as the guiding principle for juvenile justice, stressing that long sentences could hinder the opportunity for transformation.

Louisiana v. Montgomery marked a pivotal moment in juvenile justice by affirming the retroactive applicability of the Supreme Court's **Miller** decision. This ruling not only underscored the constitutional necessity of reassessing juvenile sentences but also reinforced the broader principles advocating for rehabilitation and the capability for reform among young offenders. The case has played a critical role in advancing discussions about more humane and rehabilitative approaches within the juvenile justice system, emphasizing the importance of recognizing the unique qualities of youth as they navigate the consequences of their actions.

Chapter 6: Psychological Impact of Long-Term Incarceration

The psychological impact of long-term incarceration on juveniles is profound and multifaceted, affecting not only the individual but also their families and communities. The experience of being imprisoned at a young age can result in significant mental health challenges, including depression, anxiety, post-traumatic stress disorder (PTSD), and a host of other emotional and psychological issues.

Brain Development and Incarceration

One of the critical factors contributing to the psychological impact of incarceration on juveniles is the developmental stage of their brains. Research indicates that the human brain continues to develop well into the mid-20s, with critical cognitive functions such as impulse control, decision-making, and emotional regulation maturing during this period. According to the American Psychological Association (APA), the prefrontal cortex, which is responsible for these functions, is one of the last areas to mature. This delay in brain development means that adolescents are particularly susceptible to the effects of trauma and stress, which can lead to long-term emotional and behavioral challenges.

Studies have shown that the experience of incarceration can adversely affect brain development, especially in young individuals. A study published in the journal JAMA Pediatrics found that youth who are incarcerated exhibit alterations in brain structure and may experience deficits in cognitive functioning. Additionally, research indicated that exposure to adverse environments, including incarceration, can result in elevated levels of cortisol—a stress hormone that can negatively impact brain health and development.

Emotional and Psychological Consequences

The emotional and psychological consequences of long-term incarceration are significant. According to the National Institute of Justice, approximately 75% of incarcerated youth exhibit symptoms of a mental health disorder. Common diagnoses include anxiety disorders, depression, and PTSD. The long-term effects of incarceration can lead to difficulties in relationships, employment, and social reintegration upon release.

In a report by the Pew Charitable Trusts, it was noted that young people who experience incarceration are more likely to engage in self-destructive behaviors, such as substance abuse and self-harm. These behaviors often stem from the trauma and isolation experienced during incarceration. Additionally, the lack of access to mental health services within many correctional facilities can exacerbate these issues, leaving youth without the necessary support to cope with their situation.

Recidivism and Mental Health

The interplay between mental health and recidivism is an important aspect of understanding the psychological impact of long-term incarceration. Studies have shown that juveniles who experience significant mental health issues while incarcerated are at a higher risk of reoffending once released. According to a study published in *The Journal of Adolescent Health*, youth with untreated mental health conditions are nearly twice as likely to be re-arrested as their peers who receive appropriate treatment and support.

Moreover, the experience of incarceration can impact the future choices and coping mechanisms of young people. A study by the Institute of Juvenile Justice Reform and Opportunities found that youth who are incarcerated often struggle to develop healthy coping skills due to their environment, resulting in a cycle of reoffending and further incarceration.

The psychological impact of long-term incarceration on juveniles is profound, influenced by their developmental stage and exacerbated by the stress and trauma associated with imprisonment. With the brain still maturing during adolescence, the repercussions of incarceration can lead to lasting emotional and behavioral difficulties. Addressing the mental health needs of these individuals is crucial, not only for their well-being but also for improving outcomes related to recidivism and community reintegration. Effective advocacy and reform are needed to ensure that youth incarceration systems prioritize mental health support and rehabilitation, recognizing that the long-term consequences of incarceration can be mitigated with appropriate interventions and treatment.

<u>Chapter 7: Keeping Offenders Locked in Prison: The Misconception of Safety</u>

The prevailing notion that keeping offenders locked in prison will make society safer is a complex and often misleading belief. While incarceration is intended to serve as a deterrent to crime and a means of protecting the public, research has shown that the effectiveness of long-term imprisonment in achieving these goals is limited at best. Here are several reasons why prolonged incarceration may not lead to increased safety and may even exacerbate issues within society.

1. Recidivism Rates and Reintegration Challenges

Studies indicate that a significant percentage of incarcerated individuals ultimately return to society, with many reoffending shortly after release. According to the Bureau of Justice Statistics, nearly two-thirds of released prisoners are arrested again within three years. This cycle of incarceration and recidivism suggests that simply locking people up does not address the root causes of criminal behavior, such as poverty, lack of education, and inadequate mental health support.

When individuals are released after long sentences without proper resources to facilitate reintegration, they are often ill-equipped to navigate life outside prison walls. This lack of preparation can lead to re-engagement in criminal activities, ultimately undermining public safety rather than enhancing it.

2. The Impact of Incarceration on Communities

Long-term incarceration can have devastating effects not only on the individuals imprisoned but also on their families and communities. Families often face significant emotional and financial burdens due to the absence of a member who is incarcerated. Children of incarcerated parents are at higher risk of experiencing trauma, mental health issues, and academic challenges, which can perpetuate cycles of poverty and crime.

Moreover, communities that experience high levels of incarceration often suffer from weakened social structures and increased distrust among residents. The stigma attached to having a family member in prison can further isolate individuals and families, making it more difficult for them to access resources and support systems that promote rehabilitation.

3. The Cost of Incarceration

Maintaining large prison populations is not only costly but also diverts funds away from essential community services that promote safety and well-being. Resources that could be invested in education, mental health care, job training, and community support initiatives are instead allocated to the criminal justice system. These preventative measures can more effectively reduce crime rates and enhance public safety by addressing the underlying issues that contribute to criminal behavior.

Incarceration also perpetuates a cycle of poverty among marginalized communities, as individuals frequently lose job opportunities, housing, and connections to vital support systems while imprisoned. This cycle fosters an environment where crime can thrive, undermining the very safety that incarceration seeks to achieve.

4. Focus on Rehabilitation

Evidence suggests that rehabilitation approaches—such as educational programs, vocational training, and mental health support—are more effective in reducing recidivism and promoting long-term public safety. A report from the National Institute of Justice indicates that inmates who participate in educational programs while incarcerated are 43% less likely to return to prison than those who do not.

By investing in rehabilitation rather than solely punitive measures, society can foster environments where offenders can reintegrate successfully, reducing the likelihood of reoffending and enhancing community safety. This transition supports the idea of restorative justice, which emphasizes healing for both victims and offenders.

The belief that keeping offenders locked in prison enhances public safety is a misconception that does not hold up under scrutiny. Recidivism rates, the negative impact of incarceration on communities, the financial costs involved, and the importance of rehabilitation all illustrate the need for a more nuanced approach to public safety. Rather than relying solely on incarceration, a comprehensive strategy that includes prevention, support, and rehabilitation is essential. By addressing the root causes of crime and providing individuals with the resources they need to reintegrate successfully, society can create a safer environment for all.

<u>Chapter 8: Advocacy and Reform</u>

Advocacy and Reform Needed in the Virginia Department of Corrections: Focusing on Juveniles Sentenced as Adults

The Virginia Department of Corrections (DOC) has made strides in recent years toward reforming its approach to juvenile offenders sentenced as adults. However, comprehensive advocacy and sustained reform efforts remain imperative—especially for young individuals who, due to past policies, find themselves facing disproportionately harsh sentences.

The Legacy of Recent Governors

Former Virginia Governor Terry McAuliffe set a notable precedent during his tenure by granting an unprecedented number of pardons. His commitment to addressing unjust sentences reinforced the crucial role that executive action can play in promoting justice and rehabilitation. McAuliffe's efforts aimed to provide relief to individuals who had shown growth and reform during their time in prison, particularly those sentenced as juveniles. By recognizing the potential for change, he brought attention to the human capacity for rehabilitation, advocating for a system that allows individuals to move forward after demonstrating transformation.

His successor, Governor Ralph Northam, further advanced this movement toward reform by signing legislation that made juvenile offenders eligible for parole after serving 20 years of their sentences. This critical legislative change represented a significant step forward in acknowledging the differences between juvenile and adult offenders and the importance of providing them with opportunities to reintegrate into society. However, while these changes are commendable, they do not go far enough, and more action is necessary.

Ongoing Challenges in the System

Despite the introduction of progressive programs and laws designed to support rehabilitation, significant barriers still exist within the Virginia DOC system. One of the core issues is that many individuals still incarcerated are either unaware of their eligibility for parole or lack the means to navigate the complex administrative processes that govern parole reviews. Importantly, even when a law is passed that allows inmates to be eligible for parole, this does not mean automatic release.

The parole process can be lengthy and convoluted, often taking years before an individual actually sees the benefits of legislative reforms. Inmates must actively engage with the system, submit applications, and sometimes participate in hearings, all of which can be daunting without adequate knowledge or support. This gap in understanding can lead to eligible individuals remaining in prison unjustly, serving sentences that far exceed those warranted by their actions.

Furthermore, the implementation of new laws can encounter bureaucratic hurdles that obstruct the intended benefits. When a new law is passed, it requires not just public awareness but also proper communication and support systems within the DOC to ensure that affected individuals understand their rights and opportunities. Without adequate advocacy and informational resources, even well-meaning reforms can fall short of their goals—a reality that many juvenile offenders have experienced.

The Need for Continued Advocacy

Advocacy plays a critical role in ensuring that juvenile offenders in Virginia are afforded the opportunities they deserve for rehabilitation and reintegration. Grassroots organizations, coalitions, and community members must continue to push for reforms that address sentencing laws and also provide comprehensive support systems for those navigating the complexities of the justice system.

Efforts must focus on increasing awareness about eligibility criteria for parole and expungements, creating support networks that assist individuals with legal advocacy, and establishing educational programs within correctional facilities that empower inmates with knowledge of their rights and available resources. Initiatives that focus on creating a more transparent process can lead to equitable outcomes for young offenders who have demonstrated growth and reform.

The road to reform in the Virginia Department of Corrections is ongoing, particularly for juvenile offenders sentenced as adults. While former Governors McAuliffe and Northam have made significant progress in advocating for justice and second chances, the system still requires comprehensive reform to address the barriers that persist. It is essential to understand that even when laws designed to help those in prison are passed, inmates are not automatically released; they must navigate a complex and often lengthy process to attain parole, which can sometimes take years.

Through sustained advocacy, increased public awareness, and a commitment to supporting individuals within the DOC, Virginia can move closer to a system that upholds the principles of justice, rehabilitation, and hope for all young people transitioning through the legal system. Ensuring that laws are effectively communicated and accessible will enable every eligible individual the opportunity for a second chance and a brighter future.

Conclusion and Call to Action for Reform

The Virginia Department of Corrections plays a pivotal role in shaping the state's approach to criminal justice, particularly for youth offenders. Through ongoing reforms, statistical advancements, and thorough evaluations of legislation, Virginia is making significant strides toward establishing a more rehabilitative and equitable correctional system. However, more work remains to be done. There is an urgent need for continuous assessment of laws affecting current inmates to ensure they prioritize rehabilitation over punishment, reduce recidivism, and facilitate successful community reintegration.

As advocates for justice, it is essential for community members, policymakers, and stakeholders to come together and push for transformative reforms that address the systemic issues within the juvenile justice system. We must champion initiatives that provide educational opportunities, mental health support, and restorative justice practices for all young offenders. By actively participating in this dialogue and holding the justice system accountable, we can create a more compassionate and effective approach—one that recognizes the humanity of every individual and supports their journey toward redemption and reintegration. Let us work collectively to drive meaningful change, ensuring that the future of Virginia's correctional policies reflects a commitment to justice, equity, and hope for all.

Resources for Further Information

If you are seeking more information about criminal justice reform, support for incarcerated individuals, or mental health resources, the following organizations and individuals can provide valuable insights and assistance:

1. Jason Flom, Philanthropist and Criminal Justice Advocate

  - Jason Flom is a nationally recognized philanthropist and expert on criminal justice issues. He is a founding board member of the Innocence Project and has dedicated his efforts to advocating for justice reform and supporting individuals wrongfully convicted.

  - Website: www.jasonflom.com

2. Bryan Stevenson and the Equal Justice Initiative (EJI)

  - Bryan Stevenson is a renowned advocate for justice reform and the founder of the Equal Justice Initiative, which aims to end mass incarceration and challenge racial and economic injustice. EJI provides legal representation to individuals who may have been denied fair treatment in the legal system.

  - Website: www.eji.org

  - Phone: 1-334-269-1803

3. National Alliance on Mental Illness (NAMI)

  - NAMI provides support, education, and advocacy for individuals affected by mental health issues, including those involved in the criminal justice system.

- Website: www.nami.org

- Phone: 1-800-950-NAMI (6264)

4. The Innocence Project

- This organization is dedicated to exonerating wrongfully convicted individuals through DNA testing and reforming the criminal justice system to prevent future injustices.

- Website: www.innocenceproject.org

- **Phone:** 1-212-364-5340

5. American Civil Liberties Union (ACLU)

- The ACLU addresses issues of civil rights and liberties, advocating for reform in the justice system and the protection of individuals' rights.

- Website: www.aclu.org

- Phone: 1-212-549-2500

6. Prison Fellowship

- This organization seeks to transform the lives of those affected by crime and incarceration through support services for prisoners, families, and communities.

- Website: www.prisonfellowship.org

- Phone: 1-703-481-0000

7. New Vision Organization

- The New Vision Organization works to empower individuals in the justice system and their families through educational programs, support networks, and advocacy for policy reform.

- Website: www.newvisionorganization.org

8. Virginia Coalition for the Fair Sentencing of Youth

- This coalition advocates for policies that ensure fair and just treatment of youth within the criminal justice system, focusing on legislative reforms and raising awareness about the impacts of harsh sentencing on young people.

- Website: www.vacfs.org

9. Substance Abuse and Mental Health Services Administration (SAMHSA)

- SAMHSA offers resources for mental health and substance abuse support, focusing on prevention, treatment, and recovery services.

- Website: www.samhsa.gov

- Phone: 1-800-662-HELP (4357)

10. The Sentencing Project

- A nonprofit organization that promotes reforms in sentencing policy, focusing on reducing incarceration rates and advocating for a fairer justice system.

- Website:** www.sentencingproject.org

11. Virginia Justice Alliance

The Virginia Justice Alliance is dedicated to addressing systemic injustices within the state's criminal justice system through advocacy, education, and community involvement.

Website: www.virginiajusticealliance.org

These resources can provide further insights into issues surrounding criminal justice reform, mental health support, and advocacy for the rights of individuals involved in the system. Whether you are seeking support, information, or ways to get involved, these organizations offer a multitude of options to help address and understand the complex realities of the justice system.

References

California Board of State and Community Corrections. (2022). Restorative justice: Transforming the systems. Retrieved from California BSCC website

California Department of Corrections and Rehabilitation. (2017). Youth justice division annual report. Retrieved from CDCR website

California Department of Justice. (2023). California blueprint for youth reentry. Retrieved from California DOJ website

Florida Department of Juvenile Justice. (2020). Annual report. Retrieved from Florida DJJ website

National Alliance on Mental Illness (NAMI). (2021). Mental health conditions in youth in the juvenile justice system. Retrieved from NAMI website

National Institute of Justice. (2019). Understanding the impact of trauma on youth in the justice system. Retrieved from NIJ website

Ohio Department of Youth Services. (2021). Youth services annual report. Retrieved from Ohio DYS website

Pew Charitable Trusts. (2015). Young adults and the criminal justice system: A national perspective. Retrieved from Pew website

Texas Juvenile Justice Department. (2019). Teenage rehabilitation: Transformation and outcomes report. Retrieved from Texas Juvenile Justice website

Virginia Department of Corrections. (2023). Annual report. Retrieved from Virginia DOC website

Virginia Department of Juvenile Justice. (2022). Annual report on juvenile services. Retrieved from Virginia DJJ website

Virginia Department of Juvenile Justice. (2022). Youth incarceration statistics. Retrieved from Virginia DJ website

Virginia General Assembly. (2016). Criminal justice reform bill. Retrieved from Virginia General Assembly website

Virginia General Assembly. (2019). Solitary confinement reform. Retrieved from Virginia General Assembly website

Virginia General Assembly. (2020). Second chance bill. Retrieved from Virginia General Assembly website